BIRDS OF THE ORINDA COUNTRY CLUB

By Jim Roethe

Photographs not taken by the Author were obta
at www.birdforum.com, for which the autho

The original sketch (above and on the cover) of an Acorn Woodpecker, a fam ⊃CC
resident, is by Nick Vaughn of Albuquerque, New Mexico.

THE BIRDS OF ORINDA COUNTRY CLUB
Table of Contents

BIRDS OF THE ORINDA COUNTRY CLUB

By Jim Roethe

INTRODUCTION

When I became president of the Orinda Country Club in January 2003, I seized the opportunity to combine two of my great loves—OCC and birds. It began during one of my periodic walks around Lake Cascade. As I saw the tremendous variety of waterfowl that congregate on Lake Cascade during the winter months, I began to wonder whether the membership knew about the wide variety of bird life that the Club supports. I also wondered whether anyone really cared. I decided to find out.

Over the next few months, starting with the March 2003 edition, I wrote a regular article for the *Orindan* on birds that I observed either on Lake Cascade or on the golf course. The feedback was positive and so I continued to write an article each month during my presidency and periodically thereafter. In total, I wrote 47 bird articles about 114 different species of birds found at or near OCC, all but two of which were published in the *Orindan*.

This booklet is a compilation of those 47 *Orindan* articles. I have taken the liberty of making a few edits and I have added some explanatory material. I have also organized the book by the various types of birds found at the Club. For the most part, however, the articles are reproduced verbatim. I hope that at least a few OCC members will find some pleasure in reading them. I certainly have enjoyed writing them.

On the following page is the article that started it all.

Jim Roethe   October 9, 2011

FOR THE BIRDS

Did you know that the Orinda Country Club is home to many land and water birds? On a recent walk around Lake Cascade, I saw 11 different varieties of water birds. As I began my first lap around the lake, I saw a dozen or more *Ring Necked Ducks* with their black heads and chest, light gray sides, golden eyes and gray mottled bills. This was in addition, of course, to the usual gaggle of domestic geese and *Swan Geese* and the numerous flocks of *Mallards* and *American Coot*. As I approached the turn off to La Cuesta, I saw a stray pair of *Ruddy Ducks*, the male already in its breeding plumage with his black and white head, rusty body and bright blue bill. Perched on a float in the middle of the Lake, as usual, was a single immature *Double Crested Cormorant* and a couple of *California Gulls*. On my second lap of the Lake, I spied a female *Bufflehead* and was surprised to see a pair of *American Widgeon*, the male showing its white bill, distinctive white crown stripe, green ear patch, and white wing patch. As I approached the turn near the tennis courts, a pair of *Pie Billed Grebes* caught my attention.

On other trips to Lake Cascade, one might see a number of other species of ducks, geese (*Canada Geese* for certain) or grebes. Or if you're lucky, you might see a *Great Blue Heron* or a *Great Egret* (all white with a bright yellow bill and black legs) hunting for small fish in the shallows. And in the spring and summer (assuming the new deck around our tennis shop does not solve our "swallow" problem), the sky above the Lake may be filled with *Cliff Swallows*.

More in a later *Orindan* on land birds at OCC.

March 2003

Pie-billed Grebe

Bufflehead Male

Canada Goose Pair

American Wigeon

Great Egret

American Coot

Canvasback

Common Merganser

WINTER WATERFOWL

The winter months (particularly December and January) must be by far the best time of year to observe birds at our small inland lakes and ponds. On a recent day in late December, Lake Cascade was virtually teeming with waterfowl and related birds. There were well over a hundred *Mallards* (some of them may even have been wild). Other ducks included *Ring-necked Ducks* and *Canvasbacks* (a couple of dozen each), *Bufflehead, American Widgeon, Ruddy Ducks* and what appeared to be two female *Wood Ducks*.   There were also a dozen or so *Common Mergansers* and, most surprising, four smaller, female or juvenile *Hooded Mergansers* with their unmistakable wide bushy crests flaring behind their long flat heads. There was also the largest "flock" of *Double- crested Cormorants* I have ever seen at Lake Cascade (40-50).

Why so many birds at this time of the year? For some species, Lake Cascade is merely one stop along the migratory flyway south. For others, our Lake may be their final wintering ground before returning North in the spring. In either event, we should enjoy them while we can.

February 2004

Male Hooded Merganser

Male Ruddy Duck

DIVING DUCKS

I've noted in earlier Orindans that the winter months are the best time to see migrating waterfowl at Lake Cascade—and the "diving ducks" have already begun to arrive. They will soon be present *en mass*. By the first week of November, I had already seen a dozen or so **Ruddy Ducks**, and a handful of **Buffleheads** at Lake Cascade. By print time for the Orindan, there should also be a large contingent of **Ring-Necked Ducks** and possibly a **Goldeneye** or two. These omnivorous "diving" ducks tend to be smaller than the "dabblers," and survive by diving and then swimming underwater to find their food. Unlike the dabblers, diving ducks are awkward on land (due to shorter legs) and appear to need a running start (as if they were running on water) to gain flight. The male of each species is distinctive. Except for the Ruddy Duck, each has a distinctive pattern of contrasting black and white plumage. The male Ruddy Duck has a black and white head, but its body is a ruddy brown color and its bill (during summer breeding) is bright blue. The Ruddy Duck is also sometimes referred to as a "stiff tail" duck in reference to its long tail feathers that are often cocked stiffly upright as it glides through the water looking for food below. During its dive, the Ruddy Duck uses its stiff tail as a kind of rudder to help the duck maneuver to its food source. So on your next stroll around Lake Cascade, keep an eye out for these divers.

An interesting aside: Ruddys are also unusual in that the female lays the largest eggs of all duck species in relation to its body size; seven or eight such eggs can equal the total mass of the female. Ruddy Ducks are also one of the few duck species to practice "parasitic egg laying"—laying some or all of their eggs in the nest of another Ruddy or even that of a different species of duck.

December 2005

Bufflehead

Ring-necked Duck

Ruddy Duck

SCAUP AT THE LAKE

Apropos the picture on the April Orindan Cover (spring bird arrivals at Lake Cascade), I spotted at least four Scaup on a recent walk around the Lake—a new personal first at OCC. Scaup are diving ducks normally seen in the Bay Area in the winter or when on migration. Scaup are of two types. The larger *Greater Scaup* normally stick to coastal waters where large numbers (often in the thousands) can be seen resting and feeding in local bays and inlets. Our Lake Cascade Scaup appeared to be *Lesser Scaup*—more likely to be seen on lakes and ponds than their Greater brethren, and always in smaller numbers. Both species have black heads, bluish bills, yellow eyes and white mottling on their back and sides. A close cousin to the Scaup, and a duck often seen on Lake Cascade, is the *Ring Necked Duck*—distinguished from Scaup by a white ring on their bill (that's right, their bill not their neck) and a sharp contrast between their white sides and black back and head.

By the time this Orindan goes to press, most of the migratory waterfowl seen on the Lake, including our Scaup, will have left us for their summer breeding grounds in Canada. Hopefully, our Scaup will see fit to stop through again on their way south as fall arrives.

April 2008

Greater Scaup

Lesser Scaup

Greater Scaup Pair

Compare Ring-necked Duck with ringed bill and sharp contrast on sides

WHY SUDDENLY THE GEESE?

O nce again this year, a resident gaggle of *Canada Geese* have seen fit to spend some prolonged time at OCC during the late summer and early fall months. You may have seen them at Lake Cascade or feeding on the fairways on Holes 3 or 4. Why are the geese staying longer each year on our course?

The Canada Goose is one of the West's most common and wide-spread goose, usually found in the lower U.S. during the winter months on ponds or marshes or, during the fall, in open farmland where loose grain is readily available for the taking. When we think of the great migratory birds, one of the first that comes to mind is the magnificent Canada Goose with its distinctive black head and contrasting white "chinstrap." We all remember as a child hearing the loud honking noise and looking up at the neat V- formation of the geese as they flew either north to Canada for the summer or south to the mid- and lower U.S. for the winter. Yet more and more, year round resident populations of these Canadians are showing up in our parks and on our golf courses. Why is that? It is primarily because the geese have found a special spot on their way either north or south, in a moderate climate and where food is abundant, where it is simply easier to stay put than to embark on that several thousand mile journey each year back to their normal summer or winter feeding grounds. Unfortunately, once the strong migratory instinct has left these most noble of birds, what we previously viewed from below as a magnificent migration can turn into an annoyance that must be dealt with. Here's hoping that our Canadian friends see OCC as merely a beautiful spot for a brief respite on their long journey, and that by the time this article is published they will be winging their way further south.

December 2003

Canada Goose Pair

Canada feeding – Greater White Fronted behind

WAYWARD SNOW GOOSE AT OCC

During this year's annual Audubon Christmas Bird Count, the North Orinda birders were treated to an unusual sight at OCC—a white morph juvenile *Snow Goose*—smaller than the Canada's and all white except for the typical black primary feathers and a dingy gray back and dark bill and legs. Snow Geese breed in colonies on Artic Tundra and winter on marshes and open fields in the Southern U.S, and Mexico. Wintering Snow Geese are common in the Central Valley of California and an occasional gaggle of Snow Geese can be seen flying over the Bay Area headed for places further south. Our juvenile Snow Goose was seen on Lake Cascade with about a half dozen *Canada Geese*. When the Canada Geese moved across the Lake, the Snow Goose followed. The day following the bird count, I returned to Lake Cascade with a camera and the Snow Goose was still there among the Canada flock. I snapped a few pictures and sent them to Golden Gate Audubon who confirmed that this was in fact a Snow Goose. Shortly after taking my pictures, the Canada Geese took flight with the Snow Goose right behind them. A lucky couple of days for birders at OCC.

March 2005

Snow Goose Pair in Flight

OCC's Snow Goose White Morph Juvenile

IT'S A BIRD, BUT WHAT IS IT?

At almost any time of the year, Lake Cascade yields up some real treasures for a birder. At the same time, one can see on the lake some of the most ungodly conglomerations of ducks, geese and swans on god's green earth. It seems that about half of all the year-round waterfowl on the lake are unidentifiable as a single species. Not surprisingly, bits and pieces of that notorious inter-breeder, the *"Mallard,"* can be seen in about 75% of these mixed species. The principal other identifiable "species" are the domestic *Muscovy, Graylag Goose* and *Swan Goose*. Combinations of the latter two are abundant on the lake. Perhaps most typical is the whitish to gray, goose-sized bird, sometime with a dark stripe down the back of its neck and with a black bill, atop which is a knobby protrusion. A half dozen or so are regularly seen on Lake Cascade. Even more common are the mixed species showing sure signs of "Mallard." These come in different sizes and colors. Some are duck size and some are goose size. The males all tend to have a green or dark-colored head with the familiar Mallard white stripe dividing the head from the body. Their body color ranges from white to mottled white to black to the more typical gray and reddish colors of a Mallard (and all colors in between). Perhaps most unusual, was a bird seen last year, about the size and shape of a Mallard, colored all white with a turquoise head and a bright yellow beak. Sticking out of the top of its head was a round brownish tuft of hair about an inch wide and two inches long. Only heaven knows what that Mallard got mixed up with.

March 2006

Mallard

Graylag Goose Pair

Swan Goose

Muscovy Duck

SHOREBIRDS

SHORE BIRDS AT ORINDA?

While many species of birds can be seen at the shore, when one thinks of "shore birds" one generally thinks of the sandpipers, plovers and related families. That generally does not bring to mind Orinda or the Orinda Country Club. However, I have seen at least one species of plover on the mud flat at the far end of Lake Cascade—the common *Killdeer*. While the many species of sandpipers almost always stay near the shore (except during migration), a few species of plover spend a large amount of time inland. The Killdeer may be the most common and wide spread of this group. While common on lake shores and along streams, the Killdeer also feels at home on plowed pastures, fields, large lawns and even golf courses—often far from water. If you come upon a Killdeer, you will usually know it as, when disturbed, they burst into flight and let out a loud and insistent "tyee-dee-dee," that invariably turns heads. Killdeer also remain conspicuous in flight, showing off a broad white wing bar (against a black wing tip) and a dark rufous rump and tail. The Killdeer is the only Plover to show two (rather than one) distinct black bars across its otherwise white breast. Killdeer also nest in open fields and have been known to do a convincing broken wing act if anyone approaches too near the nest. So, keep an eye out for a Killdeer—both on the mud flat of Lake Cascade and on the course.

January 2005

Killdeer on Nest

Killdeer

THE UBIQUITOUS KILLDEER

On a recent walk around Lake Cascade I was startled by the continuous sharp cry of several *Killdeer* in flight over the Lake. I have seen Killdeer on numerous occasions at Lake Cascade but never thought to write about this ubiquitous bird. It is simply too common. It is a "shorebird" that is rarely seen near the shore, preferring inland lawns, golf courses, mudflats, short grass fields and other open country. Killdeer are year-round residents in every state in the continental U.S., and breed as far north as upper Canada. They are of the Plover family—short billed birds that forage on the ground. During breeding season, eggs are laid among pebbles on open ground, camouflaged for protection against predators. Predators that do get too close to a nest are lured away from the nest by perhaps the most convincing "broken wing" act in the birding world, the parent flopping along the ground noisily until the eggs or nestlings seem safe.

The Killdeer is a particularly handsome bird—brown above and white below with a white collar and a dark double breast band below its white throat. In flight it displays a bright rufous rump and tail. Its closest "look alike" is the *Semipalmated Plover*, a smaller bird with a single black breast band that actually spends time near the "shore." And No! Killdeer to not "kill" deer. The name originates from the high pitched cry that Killdeer make in flight, thought by an early ornithologist to sound like "kil-deeeer." However the cry sounds to you, when a Killdeer is roused and takes flight, you definitely know it is present.

Not Published

Killdeer Foraging

MEA CULPA—A SPOTTED SANDPIPER AT OCC

Yikes! Only last month I told you that sandpipers "almost always stay near the shore." Then in mid-December, what did I see at the far end of Lake Cascade—a lone *Spotted Sandpiper* feeding in the mud flat. OCC member Meg Pauletich, who has led the Audubon North Orinda Christmas bird count for more years than she'd like to remember, tells me that her birders have seen a Spotted Sandpiper during the December bird count in several of the last few years, as well as a *Greater Yellowlegs* in one year (another common shorebird). Interestingly, the Spotted Sandpiper, whose breast in summer is speckled with round black spots, shows no spots in its winter plumage. It is identified by its short, stubby body, its continual bobbing motion as it forages for food and a distinguishing white wedge protruding from its white breast up onto the shoulder. Twice when I got too close to OCC's sandpiper, the bird flew across the far end of the Lake in a beeline only a foot or two above the water, using short intermittent bursts of stiff shallow wing beats—another distinguishing feature of the Spotted Sandpiper. The bird stayed at Orinda for several days, long enough to be counted in the 2004 Christmas bird count. So as I write my first bird article during the new year, I am eating a bit of crow. There are more "shorebirds" at OCC than I first believed.

February 2005

Spotted Sandpiper – Breeding Plumage

Spotted Sandpiper – Winter Plumage

Greater Yellowlegs

Lesser Yellowlegs (Note shorter bill)

GREATER YELLOWLEGS

A few weeks ago, I saw my first *Greater Yellowlegs* at OCC, foraging in the mudflats at the East end of Lake Cascade along with a *Spotted Sandpiper* and a half dozen *Killdeer*. The Greater Yellowlegs is a medium sized sandpiper (14 inches long), with coloring similar to other shorebird species—mottled brown on top and white below. It is distinguished by its long bright yellow legs and dark, slightly up curved bill. Its rarer cousin—the *Lesser Yellowlegs*—differs only in its overall smaller size and shorter bill size. Greater Yellowlegs breed in sub arctic wetlands of Northern Canada and are generally seen along the Pacific Coast only during the winter months and while in migration. They winter all along both the Atlantic and the Pacific Coasts, some migrating as far as Mexico and even Central South America. They feed on Aquatic worms and insects and an occasional small fish that they will chase down and catch in the shallow water of a mudflat or tidal puddle.

I had hoped that my Greater Yellowlegs would stick around OCC for the 2005 Audubon Christmas bird count. It would have been nice (and unusual) if we could have added a Greater Yellowlegs to the Orinda Village team's count this year. Unfortunately, bird count day brought heavy rains to Orinda chasing many birds—including my Yellowlegs—to cover. We can only hope that next Christmas will be dryer and that our Yellowlegs will find the picking's sufficiently good at Lake Cascade to make another appearance.

February 2006

A SNIPE HUNT AT OCC?

Remember as a kid when you were invited on your first "snipe hunt." It was a big joke then—usually a ploy to get a gullible friend to go exploring for some non-existent "something or other" in some desolate part of town. Did you realize then that a snipe is really a bird? Well, we have got the real thing here at OCC. During the annual Audubon Christmas count in mid-December, a **Wilson's Snipe** was spotted at the far end of Lake Cascade, foraging in the muddy shoreline. Observance of this medium sized shore bird at Lake Cascade was the first reported citing of a Snipe at OCC since the 1995 Christmas count.

Of some interest, the name of this bird was recently changed from the Common Snipe to the Wilson's Snipe. It is named after Alexander Wilson (1766-1813), often said to be the father of American ornithology. The American tradition is not to allow the discoverer of a bird to name that bird after himself. However, the discoverer can choose to honor a famous ornithologist (or a friend for that matter) by naming a new discovery after the friend or famous birder. Or, as in the case of the Wilson's Snipe, the honor can be bestowed by committee, long after the honoree's death. Perhaps those doing the honoring hope that some day in the future they may be honored by having a newly discovered bird species named after them

January 2009

Wilson's Snipe

AVOCETS AT ORINDA?

Imagine my surprise while on a brisk walk around Lake Cascade during the last week in July to see a bevy of birds at the far side of the Lake that looked an awful lot like Avocets. As I continued around the Lake to my car parked near the tennis shop, I grabbed my binoculars to get a better look during my second lap. Yes, they were *American Avocets* and there were seven of them in full breeding plumage. Some would say that Avocets are the most beautiful shore bird that we see in Northern California with their long legs, black and white body, buffy orange neck and head, and long up-curved bill. The up-curved bill is used to probe for crustaceans and other small invertebrates in mud flats and shallow wetlands.

Avocets and their close relatives the *Black-necked Stilts* are extremely protective of their young. During breeding season, if you walk anywhere near an Avocet colony the adult birds seem to go crazy. Numerous adults will fly into the air, making sharp high pitched calls, sometimes going into the broken wing act and at other times simply attacking the encroacher directly. These defensive tactics may have evolved to protect the Avocet chicks who are often born in nests amounting to no more than shallow scrapings on bare open ground near water—a relatively easy target for a wandering raccoon or fox. I have often seen Avocets all along the East Bay shoreline, but this was a first for OCC.

September 2008

American Avocet

Black-necked Stilt

American Avocets Foraging

OTHER WATER BIRDS

HERONS AND EGRETS—THE SILENT STALKERS

It is not uncommon to see a single heron or egret standing motionless along the bank of Lake Cascade, waiting for its dinner to swim by. Last month, however, I saw three different species of these silent stalkers on a single afternoon stroll around the Lake.   All three were at the far end of the Lake—a *Great Egret* (large, all white with long black legs and a sharp yellow bill), a *Great Blue Heron* (even larger and grayish-blue with a black cap) and what appeared to be an immature *Black-Crowned Night Heron* (looking much like the Blue Heron, but much smaller and with shorter legs and neck).   A few days later, there were two Great Egrets at the Lake—one hunting along the bank and the other (of all places) perched in a tree on the North side of the Lake. At other times, *Snowy Egrets* (smaller than the Great Egret and with a black bill and yellow feet) patrol the Lake. Perhaps most bizarre was the Great Blue Heron that for a week or so, perched itself on the outflow pipe sticking out of the water near the dam, apparently in an effort to see more of the Lake so as to increase its dinner menu offerings.

The "silent stalkers" are most interesting birds. They can stand motionless for many minutes, and then slowly coil their neck like a snake and make a lightning fast strike at their target—usually a small fish, amphibian, reptile, worm, crab or other "creepy crawly" along the water's edge.   An evolutionary feature of these remarkable birds finds the esophagus crossed over and lying behind the vertebrae to prevent injury to the esophagus if the striking bird hits something other than its target.

March 2007

Black-capped Nightheron

Snowy Egret

Great Egret

Great Blue Heron

THE REGAL CORMORANT

A frequent visitor to Lake Cascade is the **_Double-crested Cormorant_**. On virtually any trip around the lake you will see two or three of these regal birds, often sunning themselves on the inlet pipe in the middle of the lake or in a tree along the shoreline, with wings spread wide and head held high. On other occasions I have seen two dozen or more of these magnificent birds perched in trees along the shore. One of four species of cormorants on the West Coast, the Double-crested Cormorant is the only species that regularly frequents inland areas (some of their largest populations breed in the upper Midwest and Canada). This primarily large, black bird is distinguished from its brethren by the orange patch of skin on its face and throat. A bit bulky looking out of water, Double-crested Cormorants are superb swimmers and divers. Swimming with head and arched neck held high, they will suddenly disappear beneath the water, sometimes in a deep dive to catch a fish or crustacean, their principal food source. Some favorite breeding sites in our area are beneath the bridges crossing San Francisco Bay. Once considered endangered, the numbers of Double-crested Cormorants have been on the rise for years. Notwithstanding, the San Francisco Chronicle reports that Cal Trans will be required to spend $550,000 as part of a mitigation program to protect Double-crested Cormorant breeding sites on the eastern Bay Bridge span that is currently being replaced. Part of that cost will be to relocate nesting sites. Additional costs will result from altering construction times so as to minimize disruption of the birds during the breeding season.

May 2005

Double-crested Cormorant Sunning

Double-crested Cormorants

A SURPRISE – PELICANS AT LAKE CASCADE

Mid-October brought a pleasant surprise at OCC—two adult *American White Pelicans* at Lake Cascade. Another OCC first for me. While working out at the fitness center, Gia Vennes (a fellow bird lover) asked if I had seen the Pelicans on the lake. I said I hadn't when suddenly there they were, gliding across the east end of the lake. These majestic birds, side by side and in unison, were slowly making their way across the lake, occasional dipping their large bills into the water. Unlike there cousins the **Brown Pelican** that feed in salt water by soaring in long lines above the water and then diving into the water head first to catch fish, the American White Pelican usually fishes in fresh water in small groups— swimming slowly and occasionally dipping their bills in the water to snare their prey (small fish, crayfish and salamanders). Often White Pelicans will coordinate their effort by swimming in a line or semi-circle, slowing driving their prey toward shore where they become trapped. The Pelican's large pouch allows it to quickly scoop up as much as 10 quarts of water as it closes its bill around a fish. With wingspans ranging from 7 to 9 feet, the American White Pelican is probably the largest bird to have visited OCC. For birders, Lake Cascade continues to amaze.

November 2007

Pelican Pair

American White Pelican

Brown Pelican

Ring-billed Gull

California Gull

JUST A SEAGULL—NO WAY

There are always a few of them afloat on, or soaring over, Lake Cascade. And everyone knows what they are—they're ordinary Seagulls, of course. Not Quite! Renowned ornithologist and bird illustrator, David Sibley, has identified 27 different gull species in North America (ten or so of which reside in or regularly visit the Bay Area). Identifying species of gulls is perhaps the most difficult task for birders, and many simply do not even try. This is because gulls go through a two to four year cycle in which their appearance slowly changes from their drab (usually mottled brownish or blackish) juvenile plumage and black beak to their final adult plumage. As juveniles, identification is most difficult. Even as adults, subtle distinctions differentiate many species. And then there are the hybrids.

But not to worry. OCC's "Seagulls" are, for the most part, *Ring-billed Gulls*—the gull in our area most commonly seen away from the coast. Adult Ring-billed Gulls are relatively small gulls with white heads and bodies, pale gray backs, black wing tips, yellow legs and a broad black ring around their yellow bill. Another occasional visitor to OCC is the *California Gull*—similar to the Ring-billed Gull but slightly larger and with greenish legs and red and black marks on its yellow bill. This is the gull most often seen circling Memorial Stadium during Cal football games. A more infrequent visitor is the *Herring Gull* (a still larger gull with pink legs and only a red spot on its bill). Are you confused yet? Black headed *Bonaparte's Gulls* are said to migrate over our area, but I have never seen one at Orinda. So if you want to impress your friends, tell them that the "Seagull" they are seeing on Lake Cascade is really a Ring-billed Gull. You will most likely be correct.

July 2005

Bonaparte's Gull – First Winter

Herring Gull

A BIRDER'S ENCORE – THE CASPIAN TERN

I could not resist writing one more bird column when, a couple of weeks ago and much to my surprise, I saw what looked like a Tern fly by the window while I was exercising at the Fitness Center. I had never before seen a Tern at OCC and so was curious to confirm the bird's identity. Over the next hour while I exercised, I continued to take peaks out the window to see if the bird was still there. Several times I spotted it at the far end of the lake, white with a black cap, making broad circles 20-30 feet above the water and periodically plunging head first into the lake in the hope of catching dinner. It was definitely a Tern. After completing my workout, I drove to the far end of the lake and parked. I watched the Tern for almost 20 minutes—circling and diving, circling and diving. On closer inspection, I could see that my Tern was a *Caspian Tern*—the largest of the Tern family. I could tell by its size, thick red/orange bill and blacker wingtips seen in flight. After many years of observation, Lake Cascade continues to provide surprises.

September 2006

Caspian Tern

A FISHER IN OUR MIDST

Try to visualize things 77 years ago at OCC—a visit to the country for a picnic, a little fishing in one of the creeks or the newly constructed Lake Cascade, perhaps a short horse ride followed by a few holes of golf. It is not much like that today, although we still have the golf part, of course. We also have some active fishermen using our streams and lake, but not the human kind. I am referring to the *Belted Kingfisher* (or two or three) that make their living at OCC as professional fishers.

During last year's rainy season, I saw one of these Kingfishers on at least two occasions in the creek bed crossing our 15th Hole and running between the 16th tee and the 17th green. Then this last September, I spotted another Kingfisher sitting on the inlet valve near the Lake Cascade dam. As I continued my walk around the Lake, I saw it (or a companion) again, this time patrolling the shoreline on the opposite side of the Lake. These large-crested birds are superb fishermen that usually hunt from a branch or outcropping above a stream or lake, watching and waiting, and then plunging into the water to nab their unsuspecting prey. Unlike most other species, the female is more colorful. While the male is mostly slate-blue with a white breast and belly crossed by a single slate-blue chest band, the female has a distinctive second, rufous chest band. Our most recent visitor at Lake Cascade was the more colorful female. I wonder whether watching the birds at OCC was as interesting in 1927 as it is today?

November 2004

Belted Kingfisher - Female

Male Kingfisher with Meal

RAPTORS & WOODPECKERS

RAPTORS AT ORINDA

Perhaps the most noble of our bird species are the Birds of Prey (or Raptors). At OCC these include hawks and their close relative the falcon. Most common at Orinda is the **Red Tailed Hawk**. Red Tails are of the Buteo family—those large soaring hawks that seem to float overhead on broad, powerful wings that rarely beat, continually searching for a meal. The Red Tail's relatively short rust-red tail, flashing in the sun, makes it easy to identify. But even the Red Tail needs an occasional rest, and favorite spots include the trees along the first and third fairways.

Several smaller hawks, of the accipiter family, frequent the trees along the creek adjacent to our four finishing holes ## 15-18. The accipiters are slimmer, longer-tailed hawks that stay closer to the ground and hunt for small birds among the trees and forests. At OCC, they are either **Cooper's Hawks** or **Sharp-shinned Hawks**, two species difficult to tell apart. Both are dark above and lighter below, with long black and white striped tails. The Sharp-shinned female is about the same size as the Cooper's Hawk (14 + inches). The male Sharp-shinned is our smallest hawk—only 9 inches in length. That pile of feathers next to the 11th green—likely the work of one of our accipiter friends.

Closely related to the hawks are the falcons. The most common falcon in our area is the **American Kestrel**—a small (10 inch) but beautiful hunter that often hovers in mid-air, beating its pointed wings just enough to resist the force of the countervailing wind, searching the ground below for its dinner. A sudden "power dive" rewards the Kestrel with a large insect or small rodent. An infrequent visitor at OCC, the Kestrel prefers more open country where the winds blow stronger.

November 2003

Cooper's Hawk

American Kestrel

Red-tailed Hawk

THE MOST BEAUTIFUL OF HAWKS

It is just my opinion, of course, but I think that the **Red-shouldered Hawk** is the most beautiful of all the raptors generally seen in and around Orinda. I was thus delighted to see one crossing Miner Road adjacent to the 5th Fairway on a recent drive home.

Fortunately for us, the California race of Red-shouldered Hawks has the most distinctive coloring of all the races. The markings on their dark gray back and scapular areas are the whitest, the white bands in their tail the widest, and the rufous coloring of their breast and shoulders the brightest. It is a truly breathtaking sight to see a Red-shouldered Hawk swoop out of a tree with sunlight reflecting off its back and shoulders. The Hawk that I saw proved the point—displaying a burst of color before settling in a tree along the creek beyond Miner Road.

Red-shouldered Hawks are not nearly as common on the golf course as their close cousin the **Red-tailed Hawk**. This is because Red-shouldered Hawks prefers a forest habitat near water where they can perch in relative hiding, while Red-tailed Hawks prefers a more open habitat. Both subsist on small mammals and an occasional bird or small reptile. The California Coast and Central Valley are also the only places in Western North America where Red-shouldered Hawks can regularly be seen, while Red-tails are ubiquitous across the U.S. and most of Canada and Mexico. Aren't we the lucky ones.

April 2010

Red-shouldered Hawk

Red-shouldered Hawk Feeding

WOODPECKERS AT OCC

Did you know that there are at least six species of woodpeckers that reside at OCC? By far the most common is the **Acorn Woodpecker**. Numerous pairs of Acorn Woodpeckers live in the large oak trees along the 16th and 17th fairways and between the 18th tee and the 1st green. These noisy woodpeckers are constantly dashing among the trees, first pecking large holes in any dry branch and later filling each hole with an acorn for later use. They are the only woodpecker at OCC with a pure black back (no white mottling). Both the male and female have a bright red cap and what appears to be a yellowish white mask around an otherwise black face.

Among the large trees on the north side of Lake Cascade, you will occasionally see a **Downy Woodpecker**, a **Hairy Woodpecker** or a **Nuttall's Woodpecker** seeking insects in the tree bark. The Downy and Hairy Woodpeckers are virtually identical except for size (the Downy is 6" and the Hairy is 9") and have a white patch on their back and white mottling on their wing feathers. The Nuttall's back is black and white striped, like a ladder going up its back. Only the males have a red spot on the back of their head.

Less often seen are the **Northern Flicker** and the **Red Breasted Sapsucker**. The Northern Flicker (brown back with narrow black bars and a black chest patch) tends to stay low, feeding on insects on the ground. When flying away from you, it shows a white patch on its rump and salmon pink tail feathers. I have only seen one Red Breasted Sapsucker at OCC—along the 17th fairway. This bird has a completely red head and breast with a mottled black back. While related to woodpeckers, sapsuckers peck trees for their sap rather than to store acorns or find insects.

So as you play our golf course in the coming months, listen for the "tap tap tap" of one of these feathered friends.

March 2003

Acorn Woodpecker

Downy Woodpecker

Hairy Woodpecker

Northern Flicker

Red-breasted Sapsucker

Yellow-bellied Sapsucker

Yes, Virginia, there really are birds called "sapsuckers." During the recent Audubon bird count, we were fortunate to see a rare **Red-naped Sapsucker** at the Wagner Ranch Nature Area. The Red-naped Sapsucker generally replaces in the Rocky Mountain region the **Yellow-bellied Sapsucker** of the East. Most common in the West is the **Red-breasted Sapsucker**, a resident of OCC. I have seen the Red-breasted variety on a couple of occasions in the trees between the 16th and 17th fairways. It is a beautiful bird with a completely red head and breast. It has a white side and belly and a black back with white mottling and a white stripe on its folded wing. The unusual Red-naped Sapsucker that we saw is a bit yellowish on its belly with red only on its throat and the top and back (the nape) of its head. Unlike most woodpeckers that drill holes in trees to find insects or to store nuts or seeds, the sapsuckers drill rows of "sap wells" and later return to drink the oozing sap. As one can see from the above descriptions, sapsuckers, like many other bird species, are named simply to reflect characteristics of their appearance and behavior. The "sapsucker" name may be a bit comical, but there is nothing comical about these beautiful birds.

April 2005

AERIAL ACROBATS
SWALLOWS & SWIFTS

WHERE HAVE THE PESKY SWALLOWS GONE?

By the time you read this article we should know if our new maintenance deck around the Tennis Facilities has succeeded in ridding us of the "dreaded swallows" that made their home the last two springs in the eaves of the Tennis Shop. The swallows in question are *Cliff Swallows*, having a short square-tipped tail, chestnut throat and dark back with contrasting buffy rump. These swallows nest on the sides of buildings or under bridges in gourd-shaped mud nests with small openings at one end. Cliff Swallows are persistent birds, as our failed effort to prevent their building nests last year by stringing netting below the eves of the Tennis Shop proved. If our maintenance deck does the job this year, where might the swallows go? They could build their nests *underneath* the Tennis Shop or under one of our bridges on the golf course. Or, some other lucky resident in or around Orinda might find that our swallows have taken residence on their building.

OCC's Cliff Swallows are not to be confused with the swallows that our golfers may see in the spring and summer months swooping low over our fairways looking for insects. These swallows are primarily *Barn Swallows* or *Violet-Green Swallows*. The Barn Swallows nest in barns or sheds or under bridges in a cup shaped nest. They are distinguished by their steel blue back and forked "swallow tail" seen in flight. The Violet-Green Swallows have a flat tail but can be identified by the violet-green sheen of their backs. So don't be alarmed if a "swallow" like bird swoops near your ball on the golf course some time this spring. This does not mean a "return of the swallows."

April 2003

Barn Swallow

Cliff Swallow Collecting Mud for Nest

RETURN OF THE SWALLOWS

It has been over a year since I wrote about the *Cliff Swallows* nesting in the eaves of the Tennis Shop. Well, the swallows have returned but, as we had hoped, they have relocated below the buildings. We are thus able to continue enjoying the swallows without the mess associated with them nesting in the eaves. And there certainly is much to enjoy about these aerial acrobats. Without doubt, they are the most accomplished flyers calling OCC home—soaring high above Lake Cascade and then diving to within inches of the water as they patrol the Lake for food. At other times, they seem simply to be enjoying life as they dart among each other, often seemingly on a collision course, but always veering off at the last moment to avoid a crash. Swallows are also voracious insect eaters. As Cliff Swallows often nest near water, mosquito's and similar insect pests make up a large part of their diet. Feeding while airborne, a single Cliff Swallow consumes hundreds of insects a day to fuel its high energy activities.

In addition to the Cliff Swallows, OCC is also the summer home and/or the occasional feeding ground for *Violet-Green Swallows*, *Tree Swallows*, *Northern Rough-Winged Swallows* and an occasional *Barn Swallow*. While similar in size, feeding habits and flying ability, these close family relatives have widely varying nesting habits. The Violet Green and Tree Swallows (most often seen swooping over our fairways looking for insects), nest in holes in dead trees or in bird houses. The Northern Rough-Winged Swallows use their feet to dig nesting burrows in a hillside or the bank of a stream—sometimes five to six feet deep. The Barn and Cliff Swallows build homes of mud, often inside, on or under buildings, bridges or other man-made structures. The award for the "most elaborate nest design" must go to the Cliff Swallow—a large gourd shaped structure of mud seemingly "plastered" onto a building wall, like those we all witnessed at the Tennis Shop last summer. Once established, colonies of Cliff Swallows tend to return each year to their same nesting ground. Let's hope that is the case with OCC's swallows—*but under the tennis shop.*

June 2004

Violet-green Swallow

Rough-winged Swallow

Tree Swallow

VIEW FROM THE FITNESS CENTER

Have you tried the new Fitness Center in the Tennis Shop? What a wonderful new addition to the amenities of our "family" club. In addition to providing members with a good work out, the Fitness Center offers an added bonus: You guessed it—a chance to observe some of OCC's resident birds. On a recent visit to the Fitness Center, I was fortunate to see three different species perched on the railing right outside the window from where I was sweating away on one of the Center's twelve cardio machines. I first noticed a half dozen or so of our resident *Cliff Swallows* perched on the rail, some facing the Lake and other's facing me. A few minutes later, another swallow lit on the rail right in front of me. To my surprise, there was no buff on the neck or breast. It was not a "Cliffy" but rather a *Violet Green Swallow*, taking a rest from its seeming constant search for insects on the fairways of our golf course. Then, toward the end of my workout, a *Black Phoebe* alit. For a couple of minutes this member of the flycatcher family flitted away to catch an insect or two and then returned to its perch, before finally flying off and not returning. Other birds could, of course, be seen swimming happily in Lake Cascade. Yet it was the close-up, eye-to-eye exchange with the swallows and phoebe that made my day. It is especially easy to appreciate the beauty of these birds when you see them sitting quietly in front of you less than ten feet away.

So if a member friend says to you: "Forget the Fitness Center—I like to get my exercise out doors where I can enjoy nature," you tell her that at OCC's Fitness Center, a little bit of nature is part of the deal.

October 2005

Black Phoebe

Violet-green Swallow

SWIFTS—OUR AERIAL ACROBATS

You're upset because you just popped up your tee shot. You look up and your eyes gaze beyond the ball. If you're lucky you may see a rare visitor to OCC—one of two species of local swifts—the *Vaux Swift* or the *White-Throated Swift*. Members of the Swift family are often confused with swallows because of their similar size, habits, "torpedo" shaped body and long pointed wings. Surprisingly, they are not closely related. Swallows are "perching" birds, similar to most song bird, and can often be seen (during the summer months) perching on the outlet valve in the middle of Lake Cascade or on a nearby telephone wire. Swifts, on the other hand, have tiny feet with four short toes—all pointed forward—preventing them from perching. As a result, swifts spend almost all of their waking lives airborne—feeding, courting and even mating aloft (sometimes free-falling over 500 feet during the brief mating process). Even nest-building is accomplished primarily aloft—the Vaux Swift breaks off small twigs while in flight to build the nest. When swifts do need a rest, as in the evenings, they "roost" in colonies, clinging to the side of a tree or building.

Sadly, our visiting Vaux or White Throated Swifts are rarely seen at OCC, primarily because they feed over such a wide range and often at extremely high altitudes. Only occasionally do they drop close to land or water to feed. (The related *Black Swift*—a resident of California's Northern Sierras—is almost *never* seen except at its nest as it spends most of its time thousands of feet in the air and is known to follow storm clouds up to 300 miles to feed on insects and spiders floating in the cloud's warm air masses.) When one does see swifts, however, they are a sight to behold. Swifts are the most aerial of birds. They are usually in large colonies, chattering and skimming the treetops as they race back and forth across the sky. The White Throated Swift is reputed to be one of the fastest birds aloft. As if shot from a gun, White Throats have been estimated to reach speeds of 200 mph when fleeing a Peregrine Falcon. So the next time you sky a drive, look up. You may be rewarded for hitting that bad shot.

July 2004

White-throated Swift

Vaux Swift

THE THRUSHES

THE ELUSIVE HERMIT THRUSH

A few months ago, I spotted my first **Hermit Thrush** at OCC in the brush at the far end of Lake Cascade. The Hermit Thrush is the only brown thrush that stays in the Bay Area year round. It is also aptly named, tending to feed singly or in pairs and preferring heavy, brushy areas where it is difficult to spot.   Its small size and brown coloring also contribute to its "secretive" reputation. Actually, Hermit Thrush are inquisitive and approachable, but unless one gets exceptionally close or has a good pair of binoculars, they are often mistaken for more common birds such as sparrows or juncos.   Like other brown thrushes, the Hermit Thrush is short tailed, with a brown back and a lighter, heavily spotted, breast and a complete white eye ring. It is distinguished from other brown thrushes by its reddish brown tail. Like most thrushes, including its larger cousin the **American Robin**, Hermit Thrushes are primarily ground feeders, tending to forage in the dank undergrowth along the edge of woods.   I often hear a Hermit Thrush before seeing it. I'm referring not to the Hermit Thrush's lovely warbling song (considered by some to be the most beautiful song of all American birds), but to its constant scratching of the leaf strewn underbrush looking for insects, insect larvae, worms or snails which make up the bulk of its diet.   So when hunting for that golf ball you hit into the brush to the left of OCC's #5 fairway or to the right of #9, keep an eye out for a nondescript bird scratching for insects--it may well be a Hermit Thrush.

August 2005

American Robin

Hermit Thrush

BLUEBIRDS—Color Can Be Deceptive

I recently received a call from a member telling me that she and her husband had twice seen a completely bright (almost iridescent) blue bird fly in front of them on the 3rd Fairway at OCC. It was smaller than a robin. Had I seen it? Did I know what it was? I was surprised as I am not aware of any birds in this area that are all "iridescent blue." The **Western Scrub Jay** and **Steller's Jay** are primarily blue, but white clearly shows in the Scrub Jay in flight and both are of a duller blue and bigger than a Robin. The all blue Indigo Bunting, Blue Grosbeak and Mountain Bluebird, while the right size, are not often seen in these parts.

To my surprise, a week or so later, I also saw what appeared to be an all-iridescent blue bird cross in front of my cart as I drove up the 17th Fairway. This time, however, I thought I knew the answer as I had seen this bird on other occasions while hiking in the East Bay Regional Parks around Orinda. The bird in question is the **Western Bluebird**, a member of the thrush family. What in the spring and summer breeding months appears in flight and to the naked eye to be all bright blue, reveals its tell-tale reddish brown breast when viewed perched and through binoculars. Insects and berries make up the diet of the Western Bluebird. In the open hills around Orinda, Western Bluebirds can often be seen hovering twenty or so feet above the ground and then diving suddenly to earth to catch an unsuspecting grasshopper or bug.

August 2004

Western Bluebird

Drabber Bluebird Perched

TWO MORE FIRSTS FOR OCC

During the first week in March, I encountered two more firsts for OCC—on the bird front, that is. In the ten or so years I have been looking for birds at Lake Cascade and on our wonderful golf course, I have never before seen either a wild Turkey or a Varied Thrush. Then in a single week I saw both—the multi-colored *Varied Thrush* near the creek on No. 2 and three *Turkeys* "grazing" along the 16th fairway. What is most interesting is that these first sightings are likely due to quite different factors at play.

Varied Thrush have never been considered "rare" visitors to our area, but their numbers have varied (no pun intended) dramatically from year to year. Prior to this year, I had seen only three of these seemingly secretive winter residents during my many hikes in the East Bay. This year I have seen well over 100. In birding terms, we seem to be having what is called an "irruption" of Varied Thrush during the 2006-07 winter—i.e., an unpredictable movement of the thrush into an area in greater numbers than usual due to an unusual climate change. The Turkeys, on the other hand, are simply becoming tamer and adapting quickly to our normal Bay Area climate and can be expected to continue to increase in numbers over the years in a more predictable pattern. As an example, two years ago, I saw 3-6 Turkeys together at the Lafayette Reservoir on a couple of occasions. Last year, I saw as many as 25 together and this year I recently counted 49 together at the base of the reservoir dam on one occasion. We even have a seemingly lost Turkey residing on the streets of Orinda Downs in my neighborhood. So don't expect to see many of that most beautiful of thrushes on our course—the Varied Thrush—but those Turkeys could soon replace the Canada Goose as the bird most golfers would wish *not* to see on the course.

April 2007

American Turkey

Varied Thrush

HALLOWEEN BIRDS

Wishing all a great Halloween. Can you guess how many local birds share Halloween's traditional orange and black as their primary colors? I can vouch for at least three. Perhaps the most vivid is the *Spotted Towhee*, a resident of OCC. You may have heard the Spotted Towhee's "buzzing" sound as you passed a brushy hillside or ravine along the course. This bird has a dark black hood and back (flecked with white spots) and a rusty orange breast. Somewhat similar is the *Varied Thrush*, a late fall and winter visitor which tends to remain hidden in low brush, its black head and chest band and orange breast, throat, eyebrow and wing markings usually hidden from view. (I've not seen a Varied Thrush on our course, but have seen them in the regional parks surrounding Orinda.) And then there is the *American Robin*, "Robin Redbreast," another member of the thrush family that should be called "Robin orange breast." The male of this most common bird has a jet black head to help show off his burnt-orange breast. The *Black-headed Grosbeak* (a black and orange seedeater) and the *Bullock's Oriole* (a black and orange insect and nectar lover) are also common to our area but they have so far eluded my gaze. Let me know if you see either one on or around the course.

October 2003

Bullock's Oriole

Black-headed Grosbeak

Spotted Towhee

American Robin

SMALL SEED EATERS

THE SMALL SEED EATERS OF OCC

When I think of the small (4" to 6") seed eating birds of Orinda Country Club, the sparrows and finches immediately come to mind. Unlike the small insect eaters (June *Orindan*), the seed eaters have short, thick beaks that enable them to break open a seed's outer shell to get to the soft morsel within.

From a distance, the sparrows and finches look much alike. Upon closer examination, however, and particularly during breeding season and among the males, there are significant differences. The breeding male *House Finch* (the most common finch at OCC) is heavily striped, like some sparrows, but with bright red streaking on the head, breast and rump. At least seven species of sparrows or their related birds abound at OCC. *Chipping Sparrows*, with their chestnut cap, white eyebrow and black eye line are seen primarily in the summer. In the winter, the *Lincoln Sparrow* (contrasting gray and brown face and buff whiskers) and the *Gold-crowned Sparrow* (black head stripes and gold crown) make their appearance. Throughout the year, *Song Sparrows* (heavily streaked chest culminating in a central blotch), *White-crowned Sparrows* (black and white striped crown), *Oregon Juncos* (a gray sparrow with a solid black or slate head and chestnut sides), and *California Towhees* (large brown ground-feeding sparrow ally) can be seen all over the golf course and in the brush around Lake Cascade.

Other frequent seed eating visitors to OCC are the *American Goldfinch* and the *Lesser Goldfinch*, both bright yellow with black caps and wings (the Lesser Goldfinch also has a black or greenish back). And if you're really lucky, you might see perhaps the most beautiful seed eater of all—the *Lazuli Bunting*, with its sky blue head and cinnamon washed breast. A heart stopper for any bird lover.

July 2003

Lincoln's Sparrow

Chipping Sparrow

Lazuli Bunting

Song Sparrow

California Towhee

JUST A SPARROW—BUT A RARE ONE

During this year's Christmas Bird Count, the North Orinda count circle was one of only two in the Oakland count area to report a **White-throated Sparrow**. But it's just a sparrow, you say! True, but not one seen often in these parts—a relative rarity. White-throated Sparrows breed primarily in Canada. Most spend the winter in the Southeastern U.S. A few contrarians winter along the West Coast. It is always a pleasure to see a White-throated Sparrow in the Bay Area.

Our Christmas Count bird was seen near a feeder on El Caminito, just east of Lake Cascade. Like its fellow crowned sparrows—**White-crowned** and **Golden-crowned Sparrows**—it was feeding on the ground, picking up the scraps knocked off the feeder by other birds. These crowned sparrows almost never feed directly from an elevated feeder. They are strictly ground feeders, preferably under or near shrubs or bushes that can provide a quick hiding place should a predator approach.

The White-throated Sparrow most closely resembles the White-crowned Sparrow—a relatively drab reddish-brown bird but for a bright black and white (or occasionally brown and tan) striped head. Add a white throat and a small yellow spot above the bill and you have a White-throated Sparrow. It's simply amazing how a little patch of white and yellow can bring the broadest smile to a California birder.

April, 2010

White-throated Sparrow

White-crowned Sparrow (note lack of yellow above eye)

Golden-crowned Sparrow

OH! THOSE BREEDING MALES

What is it about the male that makes him want to stand out? The world of birds is a case in point. I received a note from an OCC member last month asking whether I had yet seen the noticeably brighter goldfinches "in heat." While the female goldfinches may be "in heat," the brighter plumage noticed by this member most likely adorned a male, doing his usual thing to show off for (and hopefully to attract) a female.   In the case of the male goldfinch, they experience in the early spring a pre-breeding molt that replaces their relatively drab winter feathers with new, bright golden plumage. This is especially true of the *American Goldfinch* that is transformed in spring to an all bright yellow body except for its black forehead, tail feathers and wing feathers (with their bold white wing bars). While the male *Lesser Goldfinch* also produces brighter yellow breast feathers in the spring, its back remains dark (either black or greenish) so that it is not quite as eye-catching as its "American" cousin.   Similarly, the common male *House Finch*, seemingly drab (pale brown) in the winter, displays a fiery red head and breast as the spring breeding season approaches. Depending on diet, the red is sometimes orange or yellow. Don't we men wish that attracting the ladies was so easy.

April 2004

American Goldfinch

Lesser Goldfinch

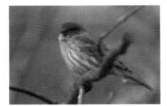
House Finch

House Finch – Yellow Variant

THE BEAUTIFUL BLACK-HEADED GROSBEAK

My books tell me that the bird is "very common in the summer in oak woods and riverside trees of the west." Yet in the several years since I took up birding, I had never seen a *Black-Headed Grosbeak*. I had seen its cousin—the *Rose-Breasted Grosbeak*—while visiting relatives in Wisconsin, but the Black-Headed variety had eluded me. Then, within a period of two weeks earlier this summer, I saw four of these lovely birds. I saw the first (a female) in Carmel in trees along a small stream where I walk my dogs. Then a week later, I saw another female in a thicket at the far end of Lake Cascade. Less than a week later, a pair (male and female) visited the feeder at my home in Orinda.

The female Black-Headed Grosbeak looks a lot like a female *House Finch* (mainly a drab gray/brown) but with a light orange breast, a distinct white stripe above the eye and white spots in the wings. The male is more distinctive with its dark burnt orange body, black head and black wings with white wing bars. The Grosbeak's closest relation is the spectacular *Northern Cardinal* (not seen in the West). Both have heavy, conical bills used for cracking or hulling seed. Grosbeaks are also known for their rich mellifluous songs. I take solace in the knowledge that Grosbeaks are more often heard than seen.

October 2004

Black-headed Grosbeak

Black-headed Grosbeak Female

Rose-breasted Grosbeak

VIEW FROM THE CLUBHOUSE

Over the last couple of months, two resident birds have caught my attention while eating at the OCC Clubhouse. A couple of months ago, over a continental breakfast in the upstairs Loggia during a meeting of the Club's Pension Committee, a female *Dark-eyed Junco* continually distracted us by bumping up against the window, evidently hoping to get in. Whether trying to reach a potential mate (her own reflection in the glass) or something that looked like food, her behavior continued for at least 20 minutes. As we were seated only a few feet from the window, the beauty of this common six inch bird became evident to all at the meeting. This was an "Oregon" subspecies of Junco. What appeared from afar to be a uniform gray turned out on close inspection to be multi-colored plumage with a chestnut back, white underside, a distinctive dark sooty hood and a pink bill. A few weeks before, on a trip to New Mexico, I was fortunate to see two of the Oregon Junco's cousins not common to the Bay Area—the "**Gray Headed**" subspecies (all gray with a small patch of reddish brown on its back) and the "*Pink-Sided*" subspecies (similar to the Gray Headed but with pinkish sides).

Occasionally, from the Grill or Oak Rooms, I have seen one of my favorite birds—the beautiful *Black Phoebe*. This small, mostly black (with contrasting white belly) flycatcher will sit on a rail or tree branch just outside the Clubhouse window. Periodically she will flit from her perch in a short zigzag flight, chasing an airborne insect. Within a second or two, dinner having been caught, the Phoebe returns to her perch to patiently wait for dessert to venture near.

May 2004

Dark-eyed Junco

Dark-eyed Junco – Oregon Type

Pink-sided Junco with Oregon

SMALL INSECT EATING BIRDS

INSECT EATING SONGBIRDS OF ORINDA COUNTRY CLUB

Word has it that my articles on the birds of Orinda Country Club have given rise to much "tittering" at or around the Clubhouse. Not surprising as the tiny *Bushtit*, the shy *Wrentit* and the melodious *Oak Titmouse* are among the most numerous of the many small insect eating songbirds that are resident at OCC.

These birds, along with such other common OCC residents as the *Ruby-crowned Kinglet*, *Bewick's Wren*, *Chestnut-backed Chickadee*, *Yellow-rumped Warbler* and *Hutton's Vireo* are recognized by their small size, melodious songs and relatively sharp pointed beaks characteristic of birds that feed primarily on insects and berries. They range in size from 4 to 6 inches and are often hard to identify as they flit about the brush or tree tops. They are more often heard than seen. But when seen, they are beauties to behold. In fact, that seemingly gray or brown bird flitting in the brush behind the 17th green, or along Lake Cascade or any of our creeks for that matter, may (upon closer inspection) show flashes of bright yellow on its wings and rump (the Yellow-rumped Warbler), or a small bright red patch on its olive green head (the Ruby-crowned Kinglet), or a black cap, white face and rich chestnut sides and back (the Chestnut-backed Chickadee). And even those small songbirds without a flash of color often display distinctive features such as the raised grey crest of the tiny oak titmouse, or the white eyebrow and downward curved bill of the Bewick's Wren. So keep your ears tuned and your eyes peeled and your golf experience may be enhanced by one of these feathery friends.

June 2003

Bushtit

Chestnut-backed Chickadee

Bewick's Wren

Hutton's Vireo

KINGLETS

Our winter Kinglets have returned from their northern summer homes where they live high in conifer forests. It seems that I cannot go anywhere today without seeing from one to a dozen *Ruby-crowned Kinglets* flitting nervously in a wooded area or thicket. But I do have to look hard to see them. Often referred to as micro-birds or "birdlets," our resident Ruby Crowned Kinglets range from only 3 ¾ to 4 ½ inches long. Its cousin—the *Golden-crowned Kinglet*—is even smaller, some measuring only 3 ¼ inches. At OCC, Ruby Crowned Kinglets can be found during winter all along any of our many creek beds, in the trees behind the clubhouse or in the trees surrounding Lake Cascade. They seem ever on the move, twitching their wings in seeming constant motion as they look for insects or insect eggs or larvae on tree trunks, branches or leaves where they forage. Both species of Kinglet are olive gray in color, with two distinct white wing bars, the lower bar edged with black. The male Ruby Crowned Kinglet has a ruby patch atop its head, which is usually concealed, but which flashes bright red when the bird is excited. The Golden Crowned Kinglet has striping on its head with both the male and female showing a yellow crown patch. While Golden Crowned Kinglets are supposedly in our area, I have never seen one at OCC, perhaps because (unlike their Ruby Crowned brethren), they tend to stay in the higher reaches of conifer forests even as they move south for the winter. I have seen them at Briones Regional Park, however, which seems close enough to OCC to count.

Ruby-crowned Kinglet

Golden-crowned Kinglet

December 2004

WARBLERS COMING AND GOING

September and October is the time of the year when birds undertake their fall migration.   During this most wonderful time for birders, we have a chance to see some bird species that are not in our area during much of the year.   Among a birder's greatest delights is to see the variety of brightly colored Wood Warblers as they move from their northern breeding grounds to warmer winter homes in the South.   And while some are leaving us for warmer climates as far south as Central America, others will spend the winter with us upon their arrival from as far north as Alaska.

David Sibley's *Field Guide to Birds of Western North America* identifies 43 species of warblers that have been seen in the Western United States.   Of the six most common in the Bay Area, three are leaving us for the South (*Yellow Warbler, Common Yellowthroat* and *Wilson's Warbler*) and three are arriving here for the winter (*Yellow-rumped Warbler, Townsend's Warbler* and *Orange-crowned Warbler*).   All six are either predominantly yellow (or a shade of yellow — olive — in the case of the Orange-crowned) or show some yellow in their feathers. On a recent search for migrants, I spotted five of the six at OCC — two of them leaving us and three new arrivals.   In the large live oak tree to the left of the first tee I saw several Townsend's Warblers and a single Orange-crowned Warbler.   And on two separate walks around Lake Cascade, I spotted a Yellow Warbler, two Wilson's Warblers and a single Yellow-rumped Warbler in the willows and wild blackberrys at the far end of Lake Cascade.   Then, on October 15 and completely unexpectedly, I was rewarded with the added bonus that all birders wish for when searching for migrants.   In a large oak tree in Ed Flynn's front yard, where La Cuesta meets Camino Sobrante, I spied a female *Black-throated Gray Warbler* — all black and white but with a tiny yellow spec in front of each eye.   For 20 minutes or so, the bird continued to forage in Ed's tree and the trees across Camino Sobrante along Lake Cascade.   This warbler probably summers to the north or east of us and winters in Mexico — a true migrant warbler just passing through OCC.

Oh yes!   I'll keep looking for the Common Yellowthroat.

November 2008

Yellow-rumped Warbler

Yellow Warbler

Townsend's Warbler

Black-throated Gray Warbler

Common Yellowthroat

In the space of a couple of weeks last month I saw two very interesting "tree creepers" at Orinda. As I began to tee off on the 7th hole, I noticed a blur on the trunk of one of the oak trees next to the tee. It was a *Brown Creeper*. But for the movement, I would have missed this Creeper as its mottled brown back blended in almost perfectly with the bark of the tree. Then a week or so later, after a brief practice session with my wife Nita on the 18th practice area (Nita was still practicing and I got bored and grabbed my binoculars and headed for the creek beyond the 17th green), I spotted a *White-breasted Nuthatch.__*The common *Red-breasted Nuthatch* may also be seen in any of the large oak trees along OCC's streams. All Creepers and Nuthatches are tree climbers. They are small birds with short tails that walk along the trunks and branches of trees, looking for insects or other goodies. While Nuthatches climb both up and down, creepers, who use their tails for support, can only go upward or sideways. They are often seen spiraling up the trunk of a tree, looking for food, and when they reach the top, flying to the base of an adjacent tree to begin the process anew.

The White-breasted Nuthatch (gray back and all white face and chest set off by a narrow black crown stripe) and the Red-breasted Nuthatch (similar but with a striped head and a red breast) will also eat seeds and are occasional visitors to Orinda bird feeders. In fact, a pair of White-breasted Nuthatch and a pair of Red-breasted Nuthatch regularly visit the bird feeder just outside my study window at home where I can watch them as I write these articles for the Orindan.

TREE CLIMBERS—CREEPERS & NUTHATCHES

Brown Creeper

Red-breasted Nuthatch

White-breasted Nuthatch

September 2004

MIRACLE OF LIFE – THE OAK TITMOUSE

This month is an opportune time to tell about an amazing event that takes place each spring about this time of year. I am not speaking about the Masters or U.S. Open golf championships. I am talking about that wondrous moment when six or so fledgling birds take their first step out of the only home they have ever known and, in a leap of faith, hop into the air and miraculously fly away. For the last several years, this miracle of life has been observed by former Club President Jeff Baus. In each of these years, a pair of **Oak Titmice** (a small, grey, crested bird and a common resident of OCC in every area of the Club where oaks and brush grow) have taken residence in a small bird house just outside Jeff's home office in Orinda. Jeff first sees the pair in early to mid-April, going to and from the bird house with bits of grass, twigs and other building materials. In a week or so, Jeff lifts the detachable roof off the bird house and, "viola," there are 6 or 7 small whitish eggs. Over the next few weeks, Jeff watches the eggs hatch and the chicks grow. Then, if Jeff is lucky, he is home on the day when, one by one, the fledglings approach the opening of the bird house and, never having had a bit of flight training, hop into the air and fly away, never to return. A post-flight peek inside the birdhouse reveals that the Oak Titmouse is a tidy housekeeper. When finally vacated, only the neat feather-lined nest can be seen in the bird house, the broken egg shells and other debris having been removed long ago by the fastidious Oak Titmouse parents. Coincidentally, I have now discovered that another pair of Oak Titmice have started a home in a small crevasse under the shingles on the side of my house in Orinda Downs. I hope that I will be as lucky as Jeff and be a witness to another of natures "miracles of life."

June 2005

Oak Titmouse

Oak Titmouse at Feeder

OTHER INTERESTING BIRDS

OCC's smallest (only 3 ¾ to 4 inches and weighing less than an ounce), but perhaps its most feisty feathered denizen, is the *Anna's Hummingbird*. The Anna's is the only year-round Hummer residing at OCC. It is also the only bird at OCC that is regularly aggressive to all other birds or animals that get in its way. One does not want to get on the bad side of an irritated Hummer. Mimicking a member of the Blue Angels, I have seen an Anna's fly straight up in the air 75 feet or so, come to a complete stop (perhaps even backing up a little), and then dive bomb straight down at a small bird that inadvertently invaded the Anna's space. The size of the offender seems unimportant to an Anna's—it can be a small bird, a large Scrub Jay or even a squirrel that has set him (usually the dominant males are most aggressive) off. Sometimes an Anna's will take after a sparrow or finch for no apparent reason—seemingly just for the sport of it. In full flight the Anna's can reach speeds of 60 mph, with wings beating up to 50 times a second. When seen hovering over a flower, the male Anna's is also beautiful to behold—metallic green above and pale below, its head and throat flashing an iridescent deep rose red when caught by the sun. Other occasional migrants to the area include the *Rufous Hummingbird*__(mainly rufous-colored on both front and back with a red-orange gorget) and the *Allen's Hummingbird* (similar to the Rufous but with a solid green back). These passers-through are usually seen in the Bay Area only fleetingly on their long migration to as far north as Alaska in the summer and south to Central Mexico in the winter. A long way to fly for such a dainty and diminutive beauty.

OCC'S AGGRESSIVE HUMMERS

Anna's Hummingbird

Anna's in Flight

Allen's Hummingbird

Rufous Hummingbird

January 2004

BLACKBIRDS OF ORINDA

"Down came a blackbird, and snapped off her nose!"

Ah! The lowly and common "blackbird," vilified in nursery rhymes as being "baked in a pie." But just what was that blackbird? At OCC it could have been one of several different species—depending primarily on its size.

Most common at OCC is the **American Crow**. During a recent 9-Tee twilight golf event, I saw at least 4 and 20 American Crows feeding on the 11th green as we ended our round and headed back to the Clubhouse. These large (19") and widespread birds often gather in flocks (as do other blackbird species) and can be seen roosting in trees at various locations on the golf course. Now and then, the Crow's cousin, the **Common Raven**, can also be seen. The two are hard to tell apart, unless seen together. The Raven's 25" size (bigger than most hawks) sets it apart. On the smaller side, an occasional **Brewers Blackbird, Brown-headed Cowbird,** or **Red-winged Blackbird** can be seen, although the Red-Winged prefer more open spaces and tend to be pushed to the countryside as human populations expand.

And finally, if you look upward, you may see soaring above our signature oak trees, a **Turkey Vulture** or two—large black birds with barely-distinguishable naked red heads—ever searching for carrion on the golf course or beyond. A close look confirms that there can be beauty in black.

September 2003

Brown-headed Cowbird

Brewer's Blackbird

Red-winged Blackbird

Common Raven

Turkey Vulture

PIGEON OR DOVE?

One of the most ubiquitous of all North American birds—what most call the common Pigeon—can be seen at OCC, but is more likely to be seen in the downtown area of any city where people gather and scraps of food are available. Domesticated worldwide for their remarkable "homing" abilities, this bird is now everywhere and of a variety of color combinations. But is the bird really a pigeon? It is actually descended from the *Rock Doves* native to rocky cliffs of Europe, and many of the local birds retain the pale gray body with two black wing bars and the iridescent neck typical of the species. So I guess it must be a dove and not a pigeon. But wait—David Sibley in his well known "Guide to Birds" refers to the Rock Dove as a "Feral Pigeon." And Kenn Kaufman in the latest edition of his "Field Guide to Birds of North America" now calls this bird a *"Rock Pigeon"* rather than a Rock Dove. Taxonomically, the Rock Dove is most closely related to other pigeons which tend to be bigger than the doves. Perhaps its closest relative is the *Band Tailed Pigeon*—slightly bigger with a light gray band on its otherwise dark tail and an obvious white neck collar, and the closest living relative to the extinct Passenger Pigeon. But it is also closely related to the *Mourning Dove*—all brown with black wing spots and a pointed tail. (Both the Band Tailed Pigeon and the Mourning Dove are also residents of OCC.)

So what are these birds—Pigeons or Doves? I say call them what you will. Both pigeons and doves are members of the same family (Columbidae) and have many similar eating and breeding characteristics. Perhaps Columbids' most distinctive characteristic is their ability to suction water into their throat without having to throw back their head to drink. They are also one of only two families of birds to feed their young "crop milk" for the first 10 days or so after their eggs hatch. So perhaps next time you'll look at that "Pigeon" with a bit more respect.

September 2005

Mourning Dove

Common Rock Pigeon

Band-tailed Pigeon

JUST FOR FUN

THE "CARDINAL"

(I originally attempted to have this article published in the November, 2004 Orindan, as my term as president of the Club was ending, but the then-editor declined, feeling that the article may be "too divisive." The next year, however, a different editor having taken the reins, the article was published — with tongue in cheek.)

I am going to go out on a limb this year and predict that the California Golden Bears will defeat the *"Cardinal"* of Stanford in this year's "big game." While meaning no disrespect to our Stanford brethren, I am convinced that we can attribute the Bears' 2004-2005 big-game success to the fact that Stanford and its fans seem still not to realize that the Cardinal is a bird, and a very beautiful bird at that. Perhaps it is the fact that this brightest of red birds is not a resident of California that has caused Stanford's confusion. Or perhaps, if I'm willing to give the peninsula team a bit more credit, Stanford recognizes that the Cardinal is a hearty and aggressive bird, even during the cooler fall season, attributes that seem to be lacking in this year's Stanford team. Whatever the reason, it is a shame that the Cardinal (the bird, that is) fails to get its due. Having recently visited the Midwest, I can attest to the beauty of a pair of Cardinals going about their business in the most hostile weather you can imagine — at times their red plumage contrasting sharply against a background of white snow. Ah, but our Stanford friends will have none of it. They say that "Cardinal" is just a color. What a shame. They don't know what they are missing. As an afterthought, it seems odd that Stanford's mascot is a tree. Have you ever seen the color "Cardinal" perched in a tree?

November 2005

Northern Cardinal

GOLF COURSES MEAN BIRDS

We spent ten days in June in the Southwest region of France with five other OCC couples on a golf outing (can you believe it, going to France to play golf). What is clear is that where there are golf courses, there are birds. And our travel gave the opportunity to see some birds not found in our area.

Of course, the French courses have their share of common house sparrows, blackbirds (two species), starlings, wrens, swallows and finches similar to OCC, and jays galore (slightly different than our Scrub Jay and Steller's Jay). They also have Robins, but their Robin, while a member of the thrush family, is about half the size of our American Robin and with only a small patch of orange-red on its upper breast and neck, extending above its bill. But the courses we played were also home to a number of new species I had never before seen, including the *Pied Wagtail, Stonechat, Blackcap Warbler, Magpie* (we do have Magpies on Sacramento Valley courses), *Song Thrush, Black Redstart* and the mysterious *Hoopoe*. Most common were the Pied Wagtails, an 8" black and white mottled relation of the American Pipit that patrolled all of the fairways and greens on the inland courses we played, searching for insects. Most unusual were two Hoopoes we saw on a links course along the coast. These 11" ground dwelling birds have a brownish-orange head looking like the exaggerated head of a Pileated Woodpecker, black and white-striped wings and a very long down-turned bill with which they hammer the ground for food. When disturbed, the Hoopoe raises a flamboyant, fan-shaped crest as it runs along the ground before exploding into a dazzling vision of black, white and orange as it takes flight. OCC may have trouble topping that.

August 2003

Pied Wagtail

Blackcap Warbler

Black Redstart

Magpie

Hoopoe

POST SCRIPT

*(This Article was written in April, 2006, after most of the other Articles in this booklet were written. It was an attempt to do some summing up. Of interest, in my various writings about the birds of OCC, I never featured two of the most common birds seen at the Club — the **Western Scrub Jay** and the **Stellar's Jay**. For the sake of completeness, I have added them to the list of "OCC Birds," in the Appendix to this booklet. It would be acceptable to omit one or two of the more obscure birds from my list, but not these two very common residents.)*

Western Scrub Jay

Steller's Jay

FINAL TALLY ON OCC BIRDS

Over the last several years I have attempted to introduce OCC members to the wide variety of bird life that co-exists with members at our beautiful Club. Perhaps it's time for a rest. But before doing that, I thought you might be interested in knowing the number of species I have seen at OCC and reported on during that time (either on the course or at Lake Cascade). The count is 78, and I am sure that if I spent three more years looking, the number would easily exceed 100. The largest bird — the majestic *Great Blue Heron* at 47 inches tall, nosing out our old friend the *Canada Goose* at 46 inches. The smallest — a tie between the *Ruby Crowned Kinglet* and *Anna's Hummingbird*, both a mere 4 inches in length. The most secretive — the single *Hermit Thrush* seen scratching for insects at the North end of Lake Cascade. The most raucous — our contingent of noisy *Acorn Woodpeckers* in the Oak Trees around the maintenance yard. (I don't count the noisy domestic geese at Lake Cascade as true "wild" birds.) The most unusual — a *Hooded Merganser* and an immature *Snow Goose*, both seen during the Christmas Bird Count in 2004. Oh yes, and the *"Cardinal"* who still doesn't seem to understand how the game is played.

If I have gotten you interested in the world of birds, buy yourself a pair of good binoculars and begin to look for yourself as you walk around the Lake or go about your activities at the Club. There is avian beauty out there just waiting to please you.

Jim Roethe

APPENDIX

The Birds of Orinda Country Club

Species	Reference Pages
Avocet, American	18
Blackbird, Brewer's	55
Blackbird, Red-winged	55
Bluebird, Western	38
Bufflehead	4, 6, 7
Bunting, Lazuli	42
Bushtit	48
Canvasback	6
Cardinal, Northern	45, 58, 60
Chickadee, Chestnut-backed	48
Coot, American	4
Cormorant, Double-crested	4, 6, 21
Cowbird, Brown-headed	55
Creeper, Brown	51
Crow, American	55
Duck, Ring Necked	4, 6, 7, 8
Duck, Ruddy	4, 6, 7
Duck, Wood	6
Dove, Mourning	56
Egret, Great	4, 20
Egret, Snowy	20
Finch, House	42, 44, 45
Flicker, Northern	29
Goldfinch, American	42, 44
Goldfinch, Lesser	42, 44
Goldeneye	7
Goose, Canada	4, 9, 10, 60
Goose/Muscovy, Domestic	4, 11
Goose, Graylag	11
Goose, Snow	10, 60
Goose, Swan	4, 11
Grebe, Pie-billed	4
Grosbeak, Black-headed	40, 45
Grosbeak, Rose-breasted	45
Gull, Bonaparte's	23
Gull, California	4, 23
Gull, Herring	23
Gull, Ring-billed	23

Swallow, Cliff	4, 32, 33, 34
Swallow, No. Rough-wing	33
Swallow, Tree	33
Swallow, Violet Green	32, 33, 34
Swift, Black	35
Swift, Vaux	35
Swift, White-throated	35
Thrush, Hermit	37, 60
Thrush, Varied	39, 40
Titmouse, Oak	48, 52
Tern, Caspian	24
Towhee, California	42
Towhee, Spotted	40
Turkey, Wild	39
Vireo, Hutton's	48
Vulture, Turkey	55
Warbler, Black-throated Gray	50
Warbler, Orange-crowned	50
Warbler, Townsend's	50
Warbler, Wilson's	50
Warbler, Yellow	50
Warbler, Yellow-rumped	48, 50
Widgeon, American	6
Woodpecker, Acorn	29, 60
Woodpecker, Downey	29
Woodpecker, Hairy	29
Woodpecker, Nuttall's	29
Wren, Bewick's	48
Wrentit	48
Yellowlegs, Greater	15, 16
Yellowlegs, Lesser	16
Yellowthroat, Common	50

Made in the USA
Charleston, SC
19 March 2012